BY

LILLY SINGH

HOW TO BE
A BAWSE

BE A
TRIANGLE

BE A
TRIANGLE

HOW I WENT FROM BEING LOST TO GETTING MY LIFE INTO SHAPE

BE A
TRIANGLE

▲

LILLY
SINGH

ILLUSTRATIONS BY
SIMMI PATEL

bluebird
books for life

First published 2022 by Ballantine Books,
an imprint of Random House, a division of
Penguin Random House LLC, New York

First published in the UK 2022 by Bluebird
an imprint of Pan Macmillan
The Smithson, 6 Briset Street, London ECIM 5NR
EU representative: Macmillan Publishers Ireland Ltd, 1st Floor,
The Liffey Trust Centre, 117–126 Sheriff Street Upper,
Dublin 1, DOI YC43
Associated companies throughout the world
www.panmacmillan.com

ISBN 978-1-0350-0276-4

Pan Macmillan does not have any control over, or any responsibility for,
any author or third-party websites referred to in or on this book.

1 3 5 7 9 8 6 4 2

A CIP catalogue record for this book is available from the British Library.

Illustrations by Simmi Patel
Book design by Barbara M. Bachman

Typeset in Adobe CaslonPro by Jouve (UK), Milton Keynes
Printed and bound in Italy

Visit **www.panmacmillan.com/bluebird** to read more about all our books
and to buy them. You will also find features, author interviews and
news of any author events, and you can sign up for e-newsletters
so that you're always first to hear about our new releases.

FOR MY MOM,

WHO IS THE TOUGHEST TRIANGLE

I KNOW.

BE A
TRIANGLE

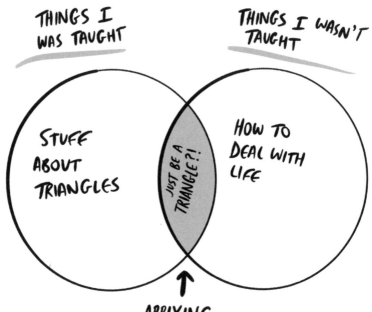

LET'S START WITH SOME REAL TALK

▲

THIS BOOK HAS TERRIFIED ME. I CONSIDER myself a hard worker, someone who puts my head down and focuses on the task in front of me. But while writing this book, I pushed deadlines, ignored calendar invites, and got really creative when it came to procrastinating. I reorganized my entire kitchen. I took out my label maker and labeled a package of Oreos with a label that said... "OREOS." You know, to avoid any possible cookie confusion. I convinced myself that that was more productive than writing this book.

Why was this book so hard to write? It's been a challenge because over the past year or two I haven't felt like the successful, happy, energetic Lilly that everyone claims me to be. In 2020, the world quite literally collapsed, my physical and mental health deteriorated, and I have a new friend who just won't leave, named Anxiety Singh.

I wanted to write an inspirational book. After

all, I'm all about hustling, and I've already written a successful self-help book called *How to Be a Bawse* (this will be the only plug for my other book, I promise! . . . you should get it). I wear power suits, baby! I'm a smiley person who always seems highly caffeinated. I knew people were going to expect this book to be a literary energy drink. So, I sat down and tried writing pages filled with what I thought I was supposed to say: mantras, tips, tricks, love yourself, quote, quote, quote, *insert the word "energy" ten times here.* And every time I sat down to write, I got lost. Day after day I would sit

at my computer and try to convince myself I had the answers for you and for me, but I simply didn't. I wasn't even the best version of myself and yet I was trying to get into Club Thrive like I belonged there. My life felt uninspiring and mundane.

And then a realization hit me like my mother's slipper. Maybe this low point was actually the perfect place from which to write THIS book. You see, THIS book isn't a book filled with ideas and thoughts I'm *hoping* will work. THIS book is filled with ideas and thoughts that are tried and tested by me and have worked. The only way to write this book was by going on the journey. And girl, was it *quite* the journey.

After all, it's pretty whack for me to try to give you ideas about how to get your life into shape when I haven't figured out how to do so myself. That would be a facade of wisdom that I generally like to reserve for Instagram, where it belongs. Catch me on the 'gram doing a staged yoga pose incorrectly any day! Plus, who wants to hear from a person who has it all figured out? Not me. I hate when I'm venting about something and someone replies with "Oh really? I don't have those issues at all." WTF, Raj? I'm not here confessing my negative feelings so that you can tell me you have positive ones all the time. I'd rather spill those feelings to Priya, who is also a hot mess, so we can try to work on ourselves together.

And that's what this book is—a chance to work through negativity together. I'm your Priya.

Wait, no. I'm Lilly. MY NAME IS LILLY. *prints out label* *labels self Lilly Singh*

I'm doing it again . . .

Recently my life has felt kind of sucky. Within these pages, I'm hoping to figure out why. More important, I'm hoping to make a lasting change, for myself and for anyone else who needs it. And so, through meditations, reflections, tough love, sunny moments, deep conversations, and 200% honesty, I have gone on the journey and written this book. Tried and tested. There is nothing in these pages that has not deeply impacted my life for the better.

I sincerely hope it speaks to your soul.

I REALLY
NEED TO BE A
TRIANGLE

▲

AS I SIT HERE AND THINK ABOUT HOW TO MAKE
life less sucky, I find myself returning to elemen-
tary school.

Minus not being able to date a Backstreet Boy,
things were simpler then. When I was faced with a
problem, a teacher taught me how to solve it. I did
homework that further developed my skills. I
would be tested on those skills to ensure I thor-
oughly understood what I had learned. And if I
continued to struggle, I would be given extra help.
My teachers really wanted me to understand the
Pythagorean theorem and damn it, they made it

happen. We made it happen. I know triangles better than I know my best friend's phone number (which I don't know at all), and I'm patiently waiting to apply that valuable knowledge in my real life. Any minute now!

Even outside of academics, all my life I've applied my problem-solving skills to whatever task was in front of me. While shooting late-night television, my crew and I faced unexpected problems every single day. An email titled "Guest can no longer make it tonight" would cause multiple departments to go into problem-solving beast mode. The talent team would put out calls for a last-minute booking. The writers would start brainstorming extra jokes to make our existing segments longer. And I would go out and improv with the crowd to buy us time. Over and over again we solved the problem because we were trained to do so. We had the skills, knew what needed to be done, and wasted no time.

Why am I telling you this nonsense? Because throughout my life—whether academically or professionally—I've faced challenges that I've met head-on. In school or at work, I not only understood the obstacles that stood in my way, but knew what the goal was once I overcame them: good grades, a degree, a paycheck, or a promotion. Although not always easy, it was always very clear and clean.

Despite all the problem-solving skills I learned, there was one major thing that I wasn't taught in school or the workplace: how to live a fulfilling life. This is not as clear and clean. In fact, I wasn't even taught that life could and should be fulfilling! I was never taught the importance of self-love, positive self-talk, happiness, or personal growth.

Growth was always measured by a grade or salary, never by an increase in compassion or patience. Not once was I encouraged to have critical conversations about the person I was or the kind of life I desired. I dissected the pain and trauma of countless Shakespearean plays in class, but I never once analyzed my own loss and heartache. At home, things weren't much different. My family was more concerned with teaching me how to clean my room

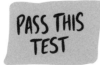

than with helping me boost my self-esteem. And did an aunty ever compliment my self-awareness like she did my outfit? No way. Why would she? My immigrant family was never afforded those luxuries either. They left behind a familiar life in India and had to learn an entire new way of life in order to survive in Canada. Between working two jobs, raising kids, learning a new language and culture, and remembering to drive on the right side of the road, there was little time to focus on what was happening in their mind and heart. As a result, no one in my family ever sat me down and gave me the "mental health talk" because they'd never heard it themselves.

The lack of value placed on mental health, and all things associated with it, during my childhood has finally caught up to me. I didn't know it then, but I know now that living a fulfilling and happy life is way more important than all of the things you learn in school, at the office, or anywhere else. We've been conditioned to believe that our skills, status, and salaries should be valued more than our happiness. Or even worse, we've convinced ourselves that these are the main things that should bring us happiness in the first place. But I don't believe that's true.

A LOT OF TIMES when I talk about living a fulfilling life and prioritizing happiness, I meet resistance, especially from an older generation. Some people, my relatives included, would consider the decision to prioritize happiness a selfish one. I know this because whenever I write about my decision to do so in an Instagram caption, my mom comments, "must be nice fool *clown emoji*." I'm kidding. My mom doesn't know how to use the clown emoji, but the rest is true.

As mentioned, perhaps my relatives felt like they never had the luxury of focusing on their desires and happiness. A salary, job, or promotion could be the difference between providing for a family and going hungry, and so there was no time to focus on anything else. And that's fair. It's important to recognize that any conversation around happiness and personal fulfillment is inevitably a privileged one. However, to this I say two things:

▲ Many members of my family have paid their dues and are now well off, comfortably able to retire and go on any vacation they please. But they seldom do. Why? Because not prioritizing happiness and fulfillment is no longer a necessity but a habit. It is this habit that I'm challenging. We must stop coming up with reasons we don't deserve a fulfilling life.

▲   I believe that living your best life is an act of service and thus should not be considered selfish. How? I'm a big believer in the idea that people who are happy and/or act with purpose make the most difference in the world. In other words, to give your best, you need to be the best version of yourself. And I don't believe you are the best version of yourself if you are unhappy or unfulfilled in life, no matter what your LinkedIn says. Keeping our full potential locked up not only does a disservice to ourselves but it does a disservice to others. If you do not serve the world in the way that only you specifically can when you are your best self, then why are you even here? We've been missing the entire point.

I have tried to do the work I was never encouraged to do as a child. I've tried to figure out how to tackle my life (because for a long time I viewed my life as an opponent rather than an ally) in order to make it the best I possibly could. But for years, I was operating at the surface level: writing affirmations on my mirror, blocking toxic people on social media, making colorful to-do lists, and writing in my journal. All of this is important, but now I feel there's a need to go much deeper and to be much more real. I was only scratching the surface because that's what Tumblr instructed me to do. I mean, I follow so many motivational influencers on Instagram—*how is that not enough?*

This desire to go deeper led me to a realization. All institutions—whether schools, corporations, or religions—have pillars of deeply embedded beliefs that keep them steady even when they are challenged by internal or external forces. The foundations of these institutions are stronger than the challenges they face. One bad teacher does not destroy the dignity of a school's mission. A disappointing sales performance does not change a company's long-term goals. Bigotry and racism do not stop people from finding serenity in prayer. What I have come to realize is that at the individual level, my core values and beliefs are not as deeply embedded as they need to be. One bad day, one failure, one broken heart, or one negative opinion could throw me off course. And I know this because I've mastered several positions in which I can cry in the shower. It's a very sad but clean Kama Sutra.

IF I'M BEING entirely honest, I'm not sure my life has *ever* had a solid foundation. I've just piled up experiences, accolades, skills, relationships, heartbreaks, and burritos into a disorganized mess. Whether my day was excellent or horrendous, I had no place to return to spiritually. Sometimes I'd teeter toward happiness, and sometimes I'd teeter toward darkness. I was just going in whatever direction life pushed me, like an upside-down triangle wobbling unstably on its point, trying desperately not to topple over.

Up until now, I've defined myself by the obstacles I have faced. I've built an identity out of my struggles. I was the girl who didn't fit in. I was the girl who was depressed. I was the girl with the family that looked different. Why did I do this? Because without a true understanding of who I

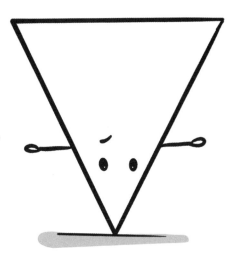

I'M FINE
I'M FINE
I'M FINE
I'M FINE
I'M FINE
I'M FINE
I'M FINE...

wanted to be and how I wanted to live my life, I defined myself by what I wasn't, because what I wasn't was very apparent to me. Without a strong foundation to steady you and a set of values to guide you, you stop being someone with limitless potential and become someone defined only by your pain. Unfortunately pain often screams louder than potential in our minds.

But I want to be more than someone who struggled with mental health. I want to be more than someone who had a rough childhood. I want to be more than someone who has felt like they didn't belong. And while I know these harsh realities will always exist as part of me, I don't want them to define me entirely.

This is where the work needs to happen. Deep down.

We need to create a home to return to. And when I say home, I'm not talking about a physical place or somewhere where pants are optional. I'm talking about a set of beliefs we return to after a day full of, well, anything. We need to dig a foundation so deep that it will exist and thrive even if our surface-level efforts fail. What is left when a harsh wind blows away my daily affirmation Post-its? What can I hold on to if a toxic person reenters my life? And what can I lean on if my journal is ripped from my hands? I need to do more than just problem-solve to overcome daily aggravations and hiccups. I have to go deeper. I have to create something strong that can withstand any obstacle, even the obstacles I haven't encountered yet. I need a belief system that is not at the mercy of my current mood. I want a foundation that stays solid no matter who is or isn't in the room and no matter what is or isn't happening in my day.

It's time to flip right side up. It's time for this book title to make sense. It's time to be a triangle.

Triangles have a wide foundation on the bottom that can support the narrow portion up top. I don't know why I just described a triangle to you, I'm sure you get it, but just in case! (Let me know if you need me to go get my label maker . . .)

An equilateral triangle pointing upward does not topple over (just ask the Giza pyramids, which have been kicking it for the past 4,500 years). When you add to a triangle, you are building upon it, without affecting its identity or throwing it off balance. When you add to the top of a square, it becomes a rectangle. When you add to a circle, it becomes an oval. When you add to a hexagon, it becomes a . . . Okay, we didn't get that far in Geometry 101. But when you add to a triangle, you do not change the essence of what it is—you simply build upon it and make it an even greater, stronger version of itself.

We must create a foundation like a triangle. That way, we can continue to grow and move through life without losing who we are. We must create a place, a system of beliefs, and a simple set of priorities to come back to should life lead us astray, which it definitely will.

I believe the foundation of our triangle needs to be made up of two seemingly simple things:

▲ A Relationship with Ourselves
▲ A Relationship with the Universe

But let's be real—the world today is loud. The world today is a Beats by Dre speaker. In a cup. Back in the day, maybe we could have gotten away with just two tiers, but not today. So, I believe we also need to include the following supporting tiers to help maintain our foundational relationships:

▲ Understanding Distraction
▲ Implementing Design

In case this is starting to feel like an LA juice cleanse, let me say (1) this book was likely cheaper than any juice in LA and (2) creating your triangle is not about finding superficial happiness. This work is not about learning how to make money, how to be a good partner to your significant other, or even how to accomplish your goals. This is more important. This is about how to build a foundation to support all of those things. I have succeeded in business. I have been a good partner. I've com-

pleted three vision boards filled with goals. And yet I've still felt lost, confused, and empty at times because I have built my life on shaky ground. I've realized it was easier to thrive in a meeting than it was to thrive in meditation. It was easier to meet someone on a dating app than it was to meet myself. And it was easier to sit in pain than to work for peace.

But not anymore. It's time to build. It's time to be a triangle.

OMG. This is the moment I've been waiting for! What I've been training my whole life for! I guess you were right, Mr. Persaud—I'm actually using triangle knowledge in my real life. Wow.

#IDidntChooseTheTrigLife
#TheTrigLifeChoseMe

Let's do this.

COME HOME TO
A
RELATIONSHIP
WITH
OURSELVES

▲

YOU ARE NOT JUST ONE THING. YOU ARE MANY things, and who you are and what you want are constantly in flux.

The first step to building a relationship with yourself is to understand who you are. How would you describe yourself? Intelligent? Kind? Stubborn? Choose three adjectives right now. Feel free to get genuine and cocky with it, but be real. So go ahead and erase "Beyoncé-esque" from your list, sweetie. This is a safe space.

My words are "hardworking," "funny," and "insecure."

I've pulled many all-nighters at work, I've told a lot of funny jokes, and after four seconds on Twitter, I've felt very insecure. But here's the thing: Although I've concluded that this is who I am, I'm not *always* these things. And you're not *always* the adjectives you just chose to describe yourself either.

I didn't work hard in my fourth year of university. I phoned it in a lot. I think I spent $1,000 on doctor's notes to defer exams because I couldn't get myself to study. I could have used that money to cover tuition for one full class or to buy half a product on Goop. That's lazy, plain and simple. Sometimes I'm just not my usual hardworking self.

I vividly remember performances when I delivered a joke with full confidence only to have no one laugh. Not even a pity giggle. Not even a lowercase "lol." Sometimes I was unfunny.

When I moved to LA, I was relentless in achieving the vision I had for myself. No matter how many times I got rejected, or failed, or felt terrified and nervous, I kept going to meetings and taking auditions, and I didn't stop believing in myself. At this point in my life, I felt entirely secure.

And that's how life is. We're never only one thing. Sometimes we're intelligent, and sometimes we're really stupid. Sometimes we're sad, and sometimes we're overjoyed. Sometimes we're great at English, and other times we isn't.

I know society loves to tell us we can only be one thing, but if the brilliant LGBTQ+ community has taught us anything, it's that everything exists on a spectrum. (Also, that love wins, but duh.)

Nothing in this world is fixed. All of us are constantly changing, and it's important to remember that two things can be true at once. You can be secure in your career and yet suffer from underlying insecurities related to your worth. You can be a genius when it comes to engineering but completely clueless when it comes to picking up on social cues. You can be fearless when it comes to jumping out of a plane but terrified of commitment when it comes to a relationship. I recently had an aunt tell me that she remembers when I was a quiet, shy young girl. Me? Quiet?! The top comment underneath all of my YouTube videos is "RIP headphone users" because I'm so loud. But apparently, when I was little I was nervous around people, and at family parties I would sit in the corner, quietly eating too much naan. Yet, somehow, I grew up to be an outspoken entertainer who thrives off an audience and enjoys being the center of attention. I went from one end of the spectrum to the other. And the thing is, as I continue to grow, I find myself returning to a place of shyness in certain environments and around certain people. My position on the shyness meter isn't a fixed one; rather, it is always shifting depending on the time and place. This is important to remember because when it comes to a relationship with ourselves, we are so quick to judge and label. We think we've figured ourselves out, but in reality we don't give ourselves credit for being complex and beautiful beings.

DESPITE THE FACT that I'm constantly evolving and always changing, society has convinced me that I must conform to a one-size-fits-all template. In fact, one of the biggest hurdles when it came to my career was the fact that I was constantly told I should get a "real job" instead of being creative and "playing pretend." Society's template tried to convince me that creativity and play are for kids and that I should grow out of them.

I can't tell you how many times I've heard my Indian elders say things like "It's too late for me," "I'm too old for that," or "This is just how my life is." And quite honestly, that has screwed me up mentally. Growing up around that energy made me think that I needed to achieve X by age Y or else it'll never happen. And that once I achieve X, I'll have X forever ever, forever ever. But this is life, not an Outkast song.

Here's what I know to be true: Nothing is forever, and you will change multiple times over the course of your life. And what you want in life will change as well. Your desires, relationships, priorities, and beliefs are constantly changing depending on what is happening elsewhere in your life. For example, years ago, I had only one desire: to be successful at my job. I spent most of my twenties hustling hard to achieve my career goals. Pulling an all-nighter to finish a project was the norm. I didn't give myself any time to socialize. And traveling across the country for half a day to attend one meeting was what I did if the situation called for it, no matter how much my body wanted a real bed. And perhaps you're expecting me to say I was miserable, but the truth is, I was so happy. I was thrilled to be all work and no play. I felt fulfilled by doing way too much in twenty-four hours. And I regret no part of it. But as I've moved into my thirties, I've realized that what I want is changing, and that's been a hard pill to swallow. I feel less of a desire to pull those all-nighters, miss those birthday parties, and make those one-day trips. For quite some time I beat myself up for it, calling myself lazy and unambitious. I was resistant to change, and I forced myself to keep doing things the way

I'd always done them. As a result, I felt unhappy and unfulfilled.

Although I still have a strong desire to succeed, my definition of success has changed over time. While I still want to achieve my goals and thrive at my job, I also want to enjoy the fruits of my labor. I want to have a break on the weekend, I want to be able to say no to something that doesn't excite me, and I want to be well rested and mentally healthy. That's not to say that I was wrong before and now

33

I'm right; it's not about right or wrong. It's that I am in a different place now and that's okay. We cannot expect to grow and also stay the same.

You are not one thing always. Nothing is ever one thing always. You are not a sad person. Your life doesn't suck. You're not hopeless. Rather, sometimes you feel sad. Sometimes your life can suck. And sometimes you feel hopeless.

People often say life is a roller coaster, but that's too simple. A roller coaster goes up, down, and upside down. Life is the entire amusement park. Sometimes you're spinning, sometimes you're chilling in the lazy river, and sometimes you're paying $40 for cotton candy you'll probably throw up anyway.

Let go of this idea that you can be easily labeled and defined. You are not clickbait on the internet. You deserve context. Change the conversation from "I'm such a stupid person" to "I'm someone currently struggling to figure out a problem I've never experienced before." We can empathize more with the second person. We can see how love and

support will help that person. We show more compassion to someone trying to figure it out than to someone we simply dismiss as stupid. We want to champion the second person. We haven't given up on them.

So yes, you are a human dealing with a set of specific circumstances that are constantly changing. And to fully embrace this relationship with yourself, you need to acknowledge that everyone else is also a human being dealing with their own specific set of circumstances. When you truly understand this, not only will you have a better relationship with yourself, but you will also connect with others in a more compassionate and understanding way.

We are all meeting each other at different parts of our journey. It's not efficient or effective to categorize people as right or wrong. What is right to you may feel wrong to someone else based on their specific circumstances, and vice versa. You could feel so strongly about issue XYZ because of what is happening in your life right now, but you need to realize that someone else can feel equally as strongly with the opposite perspective about issue XYZ because of what is happening in their life. And no matter how much you disagree with someone, it is in your best interest to empathize with where they are on their journey—not only because it will allow you to approach the situation with more perspective and peace of mind, but also because, if you sincerely believe someone is wrong, meeting them where they are can potentially help them see your point of view.

Allow me to be vulnerable and work through an example.

CLASSIC GREEN SAREE SILVER SAREE DILEMMA

(*SPOILER* THEY'RE BOTH RIGHT. #PERSPECTIVE)

At the age of thirty, I came out as bisexual to my family. It was definitely the hardest thing I've ever done in my life, and the lead-up to that moment was filled with anxiety. Out of fear that I would lose my words, I wrote my parents a letter, printed it out, and placed it in front of them. All I could muster up the courage to say was: "Read this." I vividly remember feeling a pang of guilt when my mom jokingly responded to the letter by saying, "Are you getting married?" I went upstairs while they read it, unable to be in the same room with them, and waited for what felt like an entire lifetime for anything—a knock on my door, a tap on my shoulder. After a long silence, finally I heard footsteps, and my parents entered my room.

Because I had a million thoughts and fears running through my head, I can only remember select things from our conversation. My mind simply had no more space for creating memories or computing what was being said. The only thing I can recall is that I was disappointed—their reaction was not exactly what I had expected and hoped for. The picture I took of that moment in my brain is one where I'm trying to be brave and authentic and no one is being supportive of me. That's what my mental camera captured in that pivotal moment, and that's what I believed to be true. Looking at that picture over and over again during the next two years, I let that disappointment impact my life in every way. I became less confident, harder on myself, and jaded.

After much contemplation and the reflection required while writing this book, I've come to realize that the mental picture I took of this moment was not entirely reflective of the truth. In reality, after I went upstairs, my parents came into my room and hugged me. They didn't say the exact sentences I wanted them to say, but they said many words of support. I expected perfection and instant accommodation, which isn't fair given that my parents were dealing with their own specific set of circumstances. My mom and dad grew up in a time and place where queerness wasn't discussed or openly displayed. My parents didn't have the privilege of growing up to Lady Gaga bops. I mistook their lack of experience and knowledge as disapproval. Why? Because I had grown up with a very different set of circumstances—I lived in a world where queerness was natural, ever-present, and worthy of celebration. Our circumstances were different, and without any of us acknowledging that, we let that difference come between us. That didn't have to happen. Being different humans in different circumstances doesn't mean we can't find common ground. It takes work, but the work is worth it.

It's easy to say that if the roles had been reversed, I would have reacted better and used the right words. But the truth is, I might not have. If I'd been standing in their shoes, raised in another place, in another time, I very well might have done and said the exact same things. In fact, I might have said worse. And anything else I tell myself is simply a lie. Not to mention that when I came out to my parents I wasn't just being brave. I was also nervous as hell and terrified to death. Someone could have looked at me for a split second too long and I would have chalked it up as judgment.

Even in our toughest and most heated moments, we're still just flawed human beings operating within our specific set of circumstances. And it is in our best interest to remember this reality.

Let's say someone writes a comment on my Instagram post that I think is mean. If I were in the same circumstances as that person, I might have written the same comment. If I'd just lost a loved

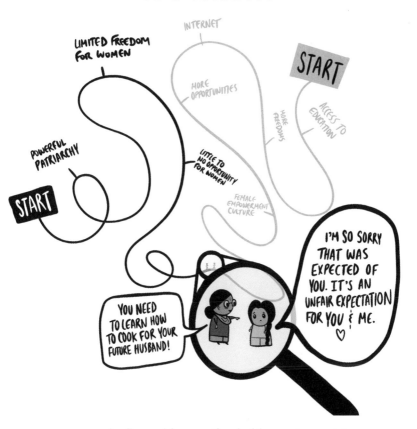

one, maybe I would get offended by an insensitive joke too. If I'd just had a horrible day, perhaps I would be unable to see the beauty in a smiling selfie. If I'd worked a fourteen-hour shift, perhaps I would feel resentment toward someone's vacation pictures. And if they were in different circumstances, maybe they would think that comment was mean too. Maybe they wouldn't even leave the comment in the first place. But we are meeting each other at different points on our journey, and that doesn't need to lead to a fight.

Being mindful of other people's individual circumstances doesn't mean people can't or won't hurt you. They will. Being mindful doesn't mean you won't get upset. You will. This isn't about being bulletproof or unrealistically understanding and forgiving. It's about reclaiming our power. People can hurt us, but rather than blame them for hurting us, we can realize we've allowed ourselves to be hurt. It's not about self-blame; it's about a nuanced, trusting, honest relationship with ourselves. People's words have definitely hurt me, but I have found more value in understanding how the circumstances I was in allowed that hurt, rather than unproductively blaming someone else for my pain. We will never control another person's circumstances, but we can always adjust our own.

After I came out, I rebuilt my confidence by

surrounding myself with supportive people, going to therapy, building myself up spiritually, choosing behaviors that empowered me, and working through forgiveness. After all, a good sign that you have a great relationship with yourself is your ability to forgive others. When you no longer need to hold on to pain caused by others or point a finger at someone else, it's because you've given yourself permission to move past what caused you pain. It's because you've changed your circumstances and you no longer operate from that place of hurt.

BE WITH YOURSELF

STRONG RELATIONSHIPS ARE BUILT AND maintained because we make time for them and prioritize them. We should do the same when it comes to the relationship we have with ourselves. We don't need to take ourselves out to an expensive dinner—all we need to do is make the time to listen.

ing what is already there. You grow because with the removal of noise, there is more room for you.

I do not believe meditation has to look the same for everyone. My dear friend Jay Shetty, a former monk, wakes up at 6 A.M. every day to meditate. You know what that makes him? Someone with a lot more discipline than me. And someone who can't make it through movie night. Another one of my friends meditates by singing. And another one by going on walks. You know what that means? I have three friends in total. But it also means that meditation doesn't require you to subscribe to an entire way of life because, at its core, meditation is simply about making time for a relationship with yourself.

I try to meditate every morning on my way to work. I listen to a certain song. I lay out my intentions and purpose for the day. I smile at other drivers, and I tap my fingers on the steering wheel. And sometimes I miss a day or two or three and that's okay. It's not all or nothing.

At home, I meditate the more conventional way whenever I can. Legs crossed, listening to music, incense stick burning (100% always concerned it'll set off the smoke detector), eyes closed. I check in with myself, ask myself questions, and work through my thoughts.

Sometimes, after an incredibly stressful day, I meditate by dancing. I play a Bob Marley song, close my eyes, and let the music move me. It's not for the 'gram. It's not for strangers at a party. It's for me to spend time with me. I feel myself move, I check in with my body, and I try to let all my tensions go.

The way you meditate is not important. Find one way (or three!) that works for you. There is no right way to do this because we are all so different. It's literally a test you cannot fail.

What should you do during meditation? It doesn't matter, as long as it nourishes the connection you feel with yourself. Don't worry about following any specific routine or agenda. Just ask yourself some questions. How are you feeling mentally, spiritually, and physically? Is something on your mind? How do you truly feel about situation

X? Are you scared? If so, why? Did you notice yourself feeling something strange last night? Did person Y make you feel excited or insecure? How can you be a good partner to yourself? What kind of day would you like to create? This is about YOU. Ask yourself what you need, and you might be surprised by the answer you give yourself.

How often should you meditate? It depends on how good a partner you want to be to yourself. Of course, the more you meditate, the more time you devote to the relationship. There's nothing wrong

NO BUT REALLY...

- HOW ARE YOU FEELING MENTALLY/SPIRITUALLY/PHYSICALLY?

- DID YOU NOTICE FEELING STRANGE LAST NIGHT?

- IS SOMETHING ON YOUR MIND?
  - HOW DO YOU FEEL ABOUT IT?

- DID PERSON X MAKE YOU FEEL EXCITED OR INSECURE?

- ARE YOU SCARED?
  - WHY?

- HOW CAN YOU BE A GOOD PARTNER TO YOURSELF?

- WHAT KIND OF DAY WOULD YOU LIKE TO CREATE?

with meditating when something is on your mind. After all, when we're sick, we take medicine. But meditation is also to the mind what vitamin C is to the body—it helps to fend off illness before it starts. So even when you don't feel stressed, meditation is helpful.

Aside from taking time to meditate—being with your thoughts in isolation—there is value in being present with yourself throughout your day. You know when you're in an elevator and for some reason it's awkward to be with someone for sixty seconds so you pull out your phone? If you think about it, you'll probably realize that you also do that when you're alone. It can be uncomfortable to be alone with your thoughts, but is that the kind of relationship you want to have with yourself? I deleted all social media apps from my phone a few months ago and started being present during dinners, conversations, walks, and cuddles with my dog. I started to be with myself, even when others were around. During a recent trip I was at the airport and every person around me was staring down at their phone. Usually this would prompt me to do the same, but instead I decided to just be present with myself. I thought about my upcoming flight, felt gratitude for the opportunity to travel, and built excitement about the adventures to come. It may sound strange, but I felt seen by myself.

Had I pulled out my phone, my mind would have been somewhere else.

So often we are in one place, but our minds are somewhere else. We are always mentally multi-tasking. We are thinking about tomorrow, or what we'll do when we get home, or how we look, or how to respond to someone, and we miss what is happening in the here and now. Wouldn't it be lovely if a conversation we were having felt like it was the only thing happening in the world? Wouldn't it be delightful if we tasted every bite of food we took instead of being distracted by thoughts of the night ahead? And how magical would it be if we got so lost in laughter that everything else went silent? Be here. Be now. Commit to the present.

The only thing you can control in this life is the relationship you have with yourself. Prioritize it, nurture it, make it the foundation of who you are. That way, no matter what new hurdles come your way each day, you can always come home to a relationship with yourself.

WHAT YOU EXPECT FROM THE UNIVERSE

WHAT YOU GET FROM THE UNIVERSE

THE UNIVERSE DOESN'T GIVE A CARE ABOUT YOUR WALLS.

COME HOME TO
A RELATIONSHIP WITH THE UNIVERSE

▲

SOMETIMES THE ENTIRE WORLD CAN FEEL LIKE it's against you and life can suck.

And it can do so in many ways. The universe is creative when it comes to finding new ways to add a little gloom to your day. It is a bittersweet artist. Paired with our tendency to believe that whatever pain we are experiencing today is definitely, for sure, the worst pain ever, that sets us up for a lifelong boxing match.

Shortly after you were born, you began teething, and even though you probably don't remember screaming and crying in agony, I can almost guarantee you did. Life sucked. It could not possibly have sucked more.

And then the universe picked up a paintbrush and got to work.

In second grade your parents didn't buy you the trendy toy everyone else at school had. You convinced yourself that the people who'd brought you into the world were somehow out to get you, that their sole purpose was to bring turmoil into your life. Stupid Mom and Dad made life suck. How could it possibly have sucked more?

And then the universe dipped its brush into a different color of paint.

In eighth grade, your parents got divorced. How dare these people? First the toy thing and now this tomfoolery? Life sucked, and that was for sure the worst.

And then the universe started to experiment with some new brushstrokes.

In your final year of high school, you failed a class. According to society, failing history in twelfth grade definitely meant you'd never get a decent job. A good job if you didn't have a thorough understanding of the Great Depression? No way. Life was so sucky, and there was no way more suckiness could enter your world.

And then the universe started to blend colors.

When you turned twenty-two, you lost your job (probably because you suck at history) and couldn't afford to pay your bills. That was definitely rock bottom, and you knew for sure things couldn't suck more.

But then they did, and sometimes they still do. The suckiness cycle repeats itself over and over again. The universe continues to create obstacles, continues to paint its complicated masterpiece. And this doesn't even take into account all the ways life can suck on a daily basis, all those little brushstrokes—arguments, parking tickets, long lines, broken escalators and printers. *Also see:* pandemics.

So yes, life can suck.

Why am I saying all this?

Because we cannot have a healthy relationship with the universe until we are honest with ourselves about the type of relationship we are in. This is the one relationship we tend to ignore the most. We miss fifteen calls from Mom but twenty-five calls from the universe.

So many of us feel like we are victims, and you know what, maybe we are, but we need to be real about what we're facing. It's foolish to think we're entitled to a life that doesn't suck. Nothing is owed to us. Why would it be? We're literally a congregation of cells that have evolved over time. Life doesn't make you any promises or sign a contract guaranteeing good behavior. Any ideas you have about what life should be are not based in reality; they're based on your imagination. So when life sucks, you are not being robbed of something that was promised to you, but rather experiencing something that doesn't meet your expectations. In other words, we tend to draw a portrait of what life looks like without ever meeting her. When she looks different from the picture we have in our minds, that's not her fault . . . it's ours. Perhaps the only thing that needs to be changed is the idealized portrait we carry around in our brain.

CONTRACT WITH
THE UNIVERSE

THIS LIFE AGREEMENT IS MADE
BETWEEN THE UNIVERSE
AND YOU.

WHEREAS THE UNIVERSE INTENDS
TO MAKE Ø PROMISES OR
GUARANTEES TO YOU AND
OWES YOU NOTHING.

SIGNED ON YOUR DOB:

THE UNIVERSE   YOU

GIVE AND TAKE

EVERYTHING IN LIFE HAS A COST. EVERYTHING.
We understand this concept when it comes to shopping, or eating junk food, or playing board games. The cost isn't always money. Sometimes it's as complex as time or as simple as four sheep during a game of Catan. That said, we often expect the

less tangible things in life to be free. But lessons are not free. Strengths are not free. Success is not free. No matter what has happened to me in my life, there's always been an associated cost. My career cost me my work/life balance, my leisure time, and often my mental health. Being great at organization cost me the ability to go with the flow. And the wonderful relationships I have now cost me years of being in bad ones.

Something horrible will often lead to something great, whether it's a lesson, a skill learned, or a layer of resilience. That doesn't mean bad things don't lead to negative feelings and situations; they very well may. But they can also, and most often do, lead to something positive, and we should acknowledge that.

Marrying your best friend now cost struggling through the brutal breakup you had years ago.

Your campaign raising $10 million for a cancer charity cost losing your father to the disease.

Having a safe, secure home cost your last house being broken into.

EVERYTHING HAS A COST

TURBAN

COST

$10/YD

JOB SUCCESS

EMPLOYEE OF THE **MONTH!**
YOU

COST

- 40+ HRS/WK
- WAKING UP EARLY
- HAVING TO PUT ON PANTS

I'm not saying these transactions are fair—or that they are right or wrong. I'm simply saying that everything is an exchange, and your relationship to the universe is no different. This is why being of service should never be undervalued. Through service, we pay our dues for all we have been given.

Would you stay in a relationship if your partner always demanded love and support but never returned it? If you always offered your ear during their venting sessions but never felt heard in return? If they kept taking and taking, never to give anything back? You wouldn't and shouldn't. Be mindful of this when it comes to your relationship with the universe. Because chances are you've been that bad partner to the universe. Maybe you just haven't noticed it because the universe didn't make you sleep on the sofa last night.

For years I would pray, look up, and ask for answers. For years I would meditate and try to summon everything good the world had to offer so I could take it with me on my day. I had one therapist tell me to "be open to the miracles of the universe," so I opened my arms every day to receive love and light. Only recently have I realized that a fundamental part of my connection to the universe is missing: what I give back to it.

You cannot only receive love and light; you also have to give it.

"not only survives, but thrives, on the gifting economy." If you've never been: Essentially, nothing is sold at Burning Man. Instead, everything—from camping supplies to food—is gifted between participants. It creates the ultimate sense of community. The chance to experience humanity at its most generous state keeps people coming back.

To be of service is to function optimally. Now when I meditate, I spend half of my time receiving love and half of my time giving love back to the universe. I think about what it is I need from the universe, and I give that very thing back. For example, if I wake up heartbroken over a failed work project, not only do I ask for the strength and guidance to overcome the hurdle, but I also send love to everyone else waking up heartbroken who may be feeling just like me because of their failed work project. I think about those who need help and how I might possibly help them. I declare that part of my purpose is to serve the world around me. I set my intention of being a good partner to the universe.

This is a partnership that will never be broken. No matter which way I refill the toilet paper, the universe and I will be partners for life. It will exist whether you choose to acknowledge it or not. No matter how many other relationships go astray, this one is in your control. So remember, no matter what new hurdles come your way each day, you can always come home to a relationship with the universe.

COME HOME TO
UNDERSTANDING DISTRACTION

▲

DISTRACTIONS CANNOT ALWAYS BE AVOIDED but they can always be uncovered.

We've established your relationship to yourself and the universe. I believe these two things are the foundation of your triangle. However, this is real life in the twenty-first century, and in this day and age, there's a lot going on. It's easy to live with clarity and purpose when you're alone on a mountain, drinking a warm cup of tea, free of aggressive bosses, nosy aunties, and thirst traps. But chances are your daily life is filled with noise and chaos. And this noise can be so loud that we subconsciously give it permission to lead us astray. That's why it's so important to understand distraction.

I'm not using the word "distraction" in the conventional sense. I'm not referring to distractions like someone talking during a movie, a dog barking while you meditate, or even the lure of a nearby party when you're stuck at home working on a project. When I talk about distraction, I mean it in the deepest sense. I define distraction as the things that take us away from the ideas, mindsets, and spaces that allow us to thrive. In other words, distractions take us away from the relationship we have with ourselves and the universe. That's why it's so important to understand distraction if we want to protect and nourish the foundation of our triangle.

A few months ago, I woke up feeling very grateful. I mean, why wouldn't I? I was fortunate to be healthy, happy, and driving to set—working another day on my dream job. And then my phone rang and it was one of my team members telling me about fifty things that were going wrong on set.

Seconds later, I hit traffic, making me late. I was sitting there idle and frustrated, thinking about how tired I was from my late shoot the day before. I didn't even have time that morning for a proper breakfast and now I was also hangry. In five minutes I'd gone from "dream job" to "why is my job so hard?" It's easy to say you should just be grateful for what you have, but it's hard to do so in the moment.

So I decided to change my thinking. Instead of chastising myself for feeling ungrateful or being upset that my job was stressful, I decided to change my mindset and think about these challenges as distractions. If I woke up grateful, then this phone call, this traffic, this tiredness, and this growling stomach were all distractions leading me astray. To manage the situation, I kept repeating, "This is a distraction from my gratitude. And you will not distract me."

We throw the word "gratitude" around a lot. As we should—it's a good word, a minimum of eleven solid points in Scrabble. But it has become a buzz-

word that has lost its gravitas. We say things like "I am grateful for your help." Or "Here are ten reasons I'm grateful today." We treat gratitude like it's a passing feeling or a trending topic on Twitter.

When we're sad, we try to remember to be grateful, but it feels impossible. We are no longer in the land of gratitude; instead we're over here in the land of expensive bills, a cheating partner, or difficult bosses. And the space our gratitude used to fill is now filled with bitterness. If we know gratitude is so important, why do we make our relationship with it so conditional? And by that I mean, why are we only grateful in certain situations or when it comes easily?

I believe we should unsubscribe from the idea that gratitude is a feeling, and instead understand it as a place, somewhere we can and should reside. We should live in gratitude and understand that anything that takes us away from it is merely distracting us. It doesn't mean these distractions aren't valid. Let's be real—problems are problems, and stress, anxiety, and pain are not imaginary. However, when we view these things as distractions from where we want to be, they seem more manageable. When we view these things as anything more than a distraction, they start to feel overwhelming and unsolvable. Distractions are little tricksters, but we can see them for what they really are. For example, the stress from my job is real, but by viewing the stress as a distraction, I'm able to get back to a place of enjoying the parts of my career that are awesome. This is a more effective thought process than simply concluding that your job is stressful and nothing else.

So no, you will not always feel grateful, and you shouldn't force yourself to. But gratitude is always the place to return to after those distractions temporarily have their way.

It's quite simple, really. If grateful is what we want to be, then anything that makes us feel ungrateful is a distraction.

Getting fired from your job is a distraction.

Your ex getting married is a distraction.

Comparing yourself to others is a distraction.

Your family not seeing eye to eye with you is a distraction.

It doesn't mean those challenges don't exist, should be ignored, or won't impact you. You will still feel heartbroken, angry, sad, or jealous, and you should allow those emotions to run their course. But you don't have to tackle these challenges while feeling miserable. You do not live in a land of distraction; you live in a land of gratitude. If gratitude is your home, you can still tackle all of life's challenges while being thankful for the chance to overcome them.

So go ahead, have a rough moment, vent about a challenge, and feel whatever you need to feel. But when you find yourself struggling, understand you don't need to stay in the land of negativity. And no matter what new hurdles come your way each day, you can always come home to an understanding of where it is you want to reside and which distractions are leading you astray.

IN A WORLD OF BENGAL TIGERS

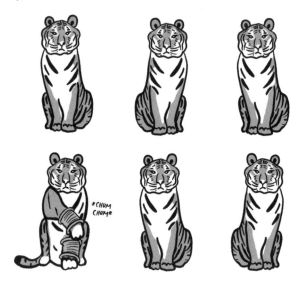

CHUM CHUM

FEEL FREE TO BE A BANGLE TIGER

COME HOME TO
IMPLEMENTING DESIGN

▲

NO MATTER YOUR PROFESSION, YOU ARE an artist in this life.

We are not born into an empty void. Sure, we talk about creating a life that is meaningful for us. We are told to "let our true colors show" and to "leave our mark on the world." But the reality is that the world we are born into is not a blank canvas. The canvas is a certain size. We've been given a certain set of brushes. And perhaps the canvas already has a sketch on it—ready to become a painting that might be very different from the one we wish to create.

From the moment we are born, we're taught certain rules. Society serves us norms, pressures, and expectations on a platter. As we grow up, most of us continue eating from that platter, never questioning what's being served to us. It's easier to follow the rules than to question them. It's easier for people to say "that's just the way it is" than to figure out a new way of doing something. And that is why we give the world permission to tell us how to be and what to do. We accept the template rather than implement our own design.

We birth a child, put them in a blue or pink onesie, and set expectations accordingly about how the child should behave.

When we watch TV or go online, we are told what is beautiful and normal. And when we don't match those images, instead of questioning the screen, we question ourselves.

We hit a certain age and feel guilty for not accomplishing all the things we've been told we should have accomplished at said age. Instead of living our life, we start playing catch-up with life.

But what if neither blue nor pink suits you? What if your body doesn't grow like the one on your screen? What if you don't want that office job? Or what if you never want to get married and have a baby?

More often than not, you will find yourself bumping up against the rules. It's up to you to decide if you will put aside your individual desires and keep eating from the platter—or break free from social expectations and design the life you truly want to live.

We must understand that the platter we are served does not always serve us. For this reason, it is in our best interest to unsubscribe from the ideas that do not work for us. To do so, we must first recognize that they are just ideas, not facts. Regardless of how hard it is and how impossible it may seem, we do have the power to choose a better, happier life for ourselves.

I am not suggesting we break all the rules and

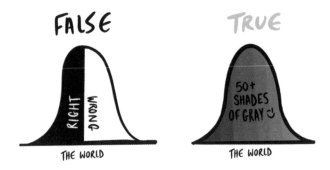

ANALYSIS
- THE WORLD IS <u>NOT</u> B+W
- THE WORLD <u>IS</u> SEXY

descend into chaos. Not everything has to be so black and white. The trick is finding the balance—a design that works for you.

Throughout my life I've had to unsubscribe from many things.

I've had to unsubscribe from ideas about what women should and should not do, especially women of color. The platter served me expectations about being quiet, reserved, modestly successful but not too successful, easy to manage, and desirable enough to win a husband's approval. If I had chosen to abide and be quiet, the world never would've heard my loud opinions on YouTube. If I'd settled for modest success, I never would've helped break any glass ceilings. And if I'd spent my energy and time on trying to gain someone else's approval, I never would've had the time to make myself proud. I didn't get to where I am by following the rules—rules created by a system that doesn't want me to win. No. That would be crazy. I got here by throwing the platter out the window. Be-

MY PREFERENCES

- ☒ SOCIAL NORMS
- ☒ OUTSIDE EXPECTATIONS
- ☒ POPULAR BELIEF
- ☒ AUNTY'S OPINIONS
- ☒ TWITTER TROLLS

☒ UNSUBSCRIBE FROM ALL

cause that is the sanest thing I could think to do. Every day, society tries to organize us and categorize us, to keep all of us following the same set of rules. Yes, some of these rules are necessary to keep humanity moving forward (please don't run a red light because "Lilly told you to"). But others exist only because people haven't pushed back against them; because people didn't question them or reject them; because no one was open enough to do something different; because progress felt uncomfortable.

When we talk about creativity, we often think about art and artists. We imagine a poet, a fashion designer, or a musician. But in reality, we're all creatives. We're all so good at creating chaos in our minds by making assumptions and overthinking. Instead of wasting that creative brain energy on maddening thoughts, we should use our imagination to design a life that fulfills us. In other words, if we can create problems that don't even exist, create fake conversations of confrontation with imaginary people while in the shower, and create anxious thoughts that keep us up at night, we can also create solutions, love, unity, and peace within us. We simply must choose to spend our energy this way.

During your meditations, when you ask yourself what you need, you will answer. Whether it's a tiny voice inside you, a pang in your gut, or a thought you can't get rid of, you will answer in some form or fashion. You will answer in the form of "I wish this was the case," or "I miss this person," or "I wish I didn't have to do this." When you have those answers, treat them like a blueprint and design a life that serves your needs. Make that the case. Reach out to that person. Stop doing that thing. It's not that easy? Well then, get creative and find a way.

At the start I mentioned that I wanted to write this book because I needed help. I need these pages as much as you do. And so, to make good on my promise, I unsubscribed from ideas that no longer serve me. To test my theory, if you will. And let me tell you, unsubscribing from these beliefs wasn't easy, but doing so has made my life far happier.

REAL THINGS I'VE DONE WHILE WRITING THIS BOOK

▲ For as long as I can remember, aging has been a point of anxiety for me. For most of my life, I've had people telling me what I should be accomplishing by a certain age—namely, marriage and

motherhood. I am in my early thirties
and for so long I have felt abnormal
and stressed because I've told myself
I'm behind. I have felt guilty because
I'm still unsure whether I even want to
bear children. I don't know what's
louder, the pressure from people around
me or the ticking of my biological
clock, but neither is helpful. I have
made the decision to look into freezing
my eggs, in case I ever want kids in the
future. I've unsubscribed from the idea
that I am required to have children or
that I need to do so by a certain age.
Instead, I have subscribed to choice, to
individual agency, to a stronger relationship with myself. And I will no
longer ignore the options available to
me just because they may be taboo for
some people.

▲ I've struggled with forming friendships
in my adult life because I've always had

a rigid idea of how friendships should look. For me to be friends with someone, I had to have known them for years, they had to have known me before I achieved any success, we had to talk every day, and we had to be nothing short of best friends forever. I kept trying to fit people into a predetermined idea of friendship instead of organically forming connections. I've unsubscribed from the idea that all friendships need to look the same, start the same way, and carry the same expectations. Instead, I have subscribed to the idea that I can have a vast array of friendships, and each one can be unique. Since then, I have formed new and loving friendships.

▲ Much of my professional success has come from saying yes to things—whether I wanted to do them or not. I believed that I would eventually earn

TRUE SUCCESS 101

LESSON 1
HOW TO SAY 'NO'

FUN NEW WORD!
PRONOUNCED: [NOH]

my stripes, which would allow me to do things my way and work solely on projects that fulfilled me. But I'd been climbing the ladder for so long, rung by rung, chasing the next thing, that I'd forgotten that my initial reason for starting the climb was to reach a point where I could make those very decisions. So lately I've said goodbye to major projects and turned down opportunities that didn't spark my interest, no matter how shiny. I've unsubscribed from the idea that success means being constantly busy. Instead, I have subscribed to the idea that success is doing what excites me.

▲ The hardest change I've made while writing this book was to my diet. I've been vegetarian for twelve years because I have ethical reservations about consuming animal products. And even though year after year I felt myself getting more and more unhealthy because I wasn't executing a vegetarian diet well, I stuck with it. After receiving recent blood test results and getting real about my health and habits, I decided to unsubscribe from the idea that vegetarianism is good for my body right now. Wanting vegetarianism to be healthy for me and it actually being healthy for me are two different things. Instead of staying on an unhealthy path, I've subscribed to working on my health and revisiting the lifestyle when the time is right. I hope I get there again. But in the interim, I've already seen positive effects.

It's been a busy few months. The growth has felt immense and the freedom is magical, though hard-earned. I continue to meditate, reflect, be present with myself, and ask myself what I need right now to thrive. And when I answer, I implement a design that serves me, no matter how taboo or outside the box it may seem. I don't care about boxes. If I did, this book would be called *Be a Square*.

So remember that you are the artist, not just the audience. No matter what new hurdles come your way each day, you can always come home to an understanding that you can design a life that fulfills you.

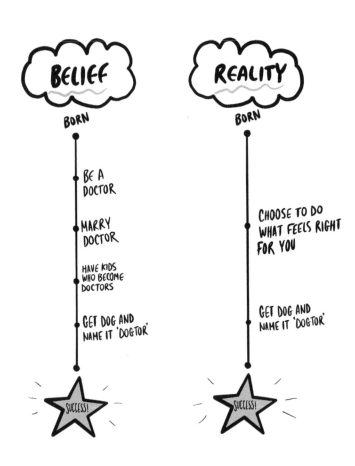

LET'S END WITH SOME REFLECTION

▲

WRITING THIS BOOK HAS CHANGED MY LIFE. I'd originally envisioned a book filled with tips, tricks, way too many pages, and lots of color. I imagined it would be a shiny product with a lot of bells and whistles. Instead, it turned out to be rather simple. And that's because this book has allowed me to shed everything that no longer serves me, to dive deep, and to get to the core of what I need and want. In writing this book, I truly found myself. And for the first time in my life, I feel a sense of genuine clarity.

Don't get me wrong—I had many rough days and moments of anxiety too. But I didn't end each day feeling as if I were staring into a void, unsure of which direction to go in, questioning who I was. Rather, while writing this book, I ended each day by returning to a place of reassurance, purpose, and comfort. I feel abundant in ways I never did before. And for that, I live in gratitude. Thank you for taking this journey with me. I sincerely hope these pages have helped create a safe space within you.

I'm sure our lives will continue to get more complex. Noise will find new ways to distract us. Heartaches and stresses will present themselves time and time again. These things will never stop. That is why we must always return to what we know to be true: our relationship with ourselves and our relationship with the universe. Everything else is a distraction. And when those distractions lead us astray, we can be creative and design a path back home to ourselves. Because we do not need to be lost. We do not need to be unhappy. We do not need to feel overwhelmed by life. We do not need to figure everything out. We simply need to be a triangle.

Be your best self and live your best life. And then share that magic with the rest of the universe.

May you receive love and light. And may you give love and light.

With my own love and light,
LILLY

ACKNOWLEDGMENTS

IN WRITING ABOUT BUILDING A FOUNDATION, anchoring oneself with a set of beliefs, and returning home to what serves us, I've become excited about a life in which I continuously implement my own words. That said, I can't help but think of the times, before I wrote this book, when my foundation was crumbling, I struggled to believe in anything, and I was uncertain about where home was for me. In those moments, there were always people who let me lean on their triangle while I tried to build my own.

Thank you to my family for constantly handling the curveballs I throw your way. You are so deeply part of everything I do. To my mom, dad, and sister, I love you dearly. Any work I do to improve myself is not only for me, but also to bring the best version of myself to our relationship.

To my chosen family and friends, thank you for nurturing me and celebrating every part of me. Double thanks for tolerating me at my most annoying points, of which I am sure there are many. I hope to be a light in your lives as so many of you have been for me. Specifically, thank you (and sorry) to Audrie and Humble for being my therapists before I hired an actual therapist.

Thank you to my entire team who works tirelessly behind the scenes to ensure I can do extraordinary things like write a book. Or two. So much of my life is beyond my wildest dreams, and it is because you believe in me. Thank you, Kyle, not only for ensuring that my career flourishes, but for also placing value in my heart, mind, and wellbeing.

While writing this book, I thought, "Wow, I'm a really rational, mature adult." And now I'm going to either prove that or diminish that, depending on your perspective, by sincerely thanking my dog. Scarbro, you are my best friend. Thank you for sitting on my lap while I wrote these pages. You're such a good boy.

And of course, thanks to you, my reader. Every single part of my career has been made possible because people tuned in, subscribed, followed, supported, and ordered. Thank you for allowing me into your space and day. I know your time and energy are valuable and limited and I am honored. I hope we can stay connected.

Thank you. A million times over.

An author, actress, and creator, LILLY SINGH brings a message of positivity and mindfulness to her global audience. Singh has found worldwide fame through her comedic and inspirational content, amassing nearly forty million followers across her social media channels alongside projects with major Hollywood studios via her production company Unicorn Island. A native of Toronto, Singh lives in Los Angeles. She is proudly of Punjabi descent.

ABOUT THE TYPE

This book was set in Caslon, a typeface first designed in 1722 by William Caslon (1692–1766). Its widespread use by most English printers in the early eighteenth century soon supplanted the Dutch typefaces that had formerly prevailed. The roman is considered a "workhorse" typeface due to its pleasant, open appearance, while the italic is exceedingly decorative.

**This book is to be returned on or before
the last date stamped below.**

11. APR. 2000

MARSTON